FINDING YOUR

GERMAN

ANCESTORS

A Beginner's Guide

FINDING YOUR GERMAN ANCESTORS

A Beginner's Guide

Kevan M. Hansen

Ancestry.

Library of Congress Cataloging-in-Publication Data

Hansen, Kevan M., 1962-
Finding your German ancestry / Kevan M. Hansen.
p. cm.
Includes bibliographical references and index.
ISBN 0-91-64898-3 (softcover)
1. German Americans--Genealogy--handbooks, manuals, etc.
2. Germany--Genealogy--handbooks, manuals, etc. I. Title.
E184.G3 H2346 1998
929' .1' 08931073--dc21

98-48538
CIP

Copyright ©1999
Ancestry.com Incorporated
P.O. Box 990
Orem, Utah 84059
www.ancestry.com

First Printing 1999
10 9 8 7 6 5 4 3 2 1

Printed in the United States of America

www.ancestry.com

Cover: Interior Mosaic, Kaiser Wilhelm Church.

CONTENTS

List of Illustrations:

ꟷNTRODUCTION

HIS BOOK PROVIDES an introduction for researchers who have not previously worked with German records, and it highlights some excellent sources for researchers who have become excited by genealogy in the United States but have "cold feet" about researching in Germany. It is assumed that researchers have identified a location in Germany and are eager to begin working in German records. Before initiating research in German records, researchers who have only general information about their ancestors' place of origin should dig deeper to discover where in Germany their ancestors settled. This knowledge will prevent the disappointment of failing to find an ancestor and will ensure that research in German sources will proceed from a solid base.

Due to the continual changes of boundaries and jurisdictions in historic Germany (discussed in chapter 1), the types of records available vary from region to region in today's Germany. Researchers who learn as much as possible about the area of their ancestors' origin will not only have a greater understanding of their lives but will gain a tremendous asset in understanding the records of the area. Chapter 2 explains the current locations of records from regions with names and boundaries that have changed.

Any foreign language is intimidating to many researchers when they are trying to learn about new sources; however, the right tools (discussed in chapter 2) enable researchers to master the skills necessary to work comfortably with foreign records. German records that initially seemed so intimidating, soon will seem like old friends.

This book is not intended to be a comprehensive source for researchers of German records. While chapter 3 introduces the various types of records (church, vital, land, court, etc.), it touches on each only briefly. Chapters 4–6 provide addresses and contact information for record repositories and genealogical societies in Germany.

I hope that the information presented will spark an interest in researchers who have wavered on beginning to investigate German ancestry. Those who stretch their knowledge and explore the numerous resources available will find a greater appreciation for their ancestors and the German blood they pass to their descendants.

CHAPTER ONE

HISTORIC GERMANY

IT WOULD NOT be unusual for a researcher new to German records to apply prior experience with searching United States sources in approaching German sources. However, a researcher may become frustrated in finding that many of the records sought do not exist in Germany. To access the records of greatest value, it is essential to identify a town or district. It may come as a great surprise that a country covering less area than the state of Illinois has none of the national sources one might expect.

For researchers who do not know a specific locale, this lack of knowledge often becomes an obstacle that cannot be overcome without further work in United States sources. Even those who have approached their research armed with a specific town name may be frustrated in locating the records because the location they seek is now within the boundaries of another country. The following overview of the area we know today as Germany should provide a basis for understanding the nature of German records. Later chapters provide specifics on which records to search, the information to be obtained from them, and help in finding their present location.

ᗩNCIENT ᕼISTORY

The earliest history of the area we know as Germany was influenced by the Roman Empire, which had become the central power in western Europe. Between 100 and 200 B.C. the Romans had slowly forced their influence northward into areas occupied by modern regions of southern Germany and France. Simultaneously, Germanic tribes, or barbarians as the Romans knew them, began to move south and west into areas along the Roman frontier. This region, largely defined by the Danube and Rhine Rivers, suffered several incursions by the Romans in the decades prior to 9 A.D.

The Germanic tribes had suffered many defeats during the reign of Julius Caesar but had never been subjugated by the Romans. In 9 A.D., during the reign of Caesar Augustus, the Germanic tribes along the Roman border rose in rebellion under the leadership of their chief, Hermann. Pressing the attack against the Roman legions along the Rhine River, they drove the army into the surrounding forest. In a battle that lasted three days, the Roman troops were surrounded and completely exterminated along with their commander, Varus. This proved to be the only serious war fought during Augustus' rule.

Had the Germanic invaders continued their advance against Rome, our version of German history might have been much different. Instead, constant conflict among the Germanic tribes, as is common throughout much of German history, allowed the Romans to regroup and fortify their borders along the Rhine and Danube frontiers. Although this put an end to Rome's attempts at expansion along these borders, the Romans continued to combat Germanic raids.

During the fifth century, the Roman Empire began to weaken due to internal conflicts and challenges to its power throughout the empire. As a result of its weakened state, the various Germanic tribes migrated freely through the Roman frontier, ending Roman power in the west.

As these areas were settled, the various tribes and clans banded together, forming larger groups that ruled over their own lands. The four largest groups, which became the basis of our German ancestors, were the Franks in the west, the Saxons in the central regions, the Allemanen or Swabians in the central and southeast areas, and the Bavarians in the south.

RISE OF FRANKISH POWER

The Franks comprised one of the largest related groups of tribes. They extended their holdings through military conquest, thereby bringing many other tribes under their rule. Their expansion included areas in modern France, Belgium, the Netherlands, and some areas of Germany.

In the late fifth century, under the leadership of the Merovingian King Clovis I, the Franks were able to defeat local Roman leaders and unite many of the Germanic tribes. In this manner, they were able to replace the Roman Empire as the dominating force in much of western Europe.

Under Clovis' leadership, some Roman social practices and laws were introduced to the people of the Frankish Empire. In 496 A.D., Clovis converted to Christianity and was instrumental in spreading the Roman religion to the empire by establishing churches and monasteries.

In the ensuing centuries, successive Merovingian kings weakened the Franks' power over this area. It was not until the rise of Charles Martel, a court councilor, that strong rule again was asserted. Charles led the Franks to successive military victories, culminating at the Battle of Poitiers in 732 A.D. Although he was a strong leader, Charles Martel never assumed the leadership of the kingdom. The overthrow of the Merovingian rulers was left to Charles' son, Pepin the Short. His rule marked the beginning of the Carolingian Dynasty. Under his leadership, the Franks were again united under a strong ruler.

When Pepin's son, Karl der Grosse, assumed leadership in 768 A.D., the empire of the Franks again began to expand. Through military conquest, Karl, better known as Charlemagne, brought the majority of Europe under his administration. This allowed the spread of the church throughout this vast area that included lands in modern France, Austria, Switzerland, and Germany. On Christmas Day, 800 A.D., Pope Leo III crowned Charlemagne emperor, thereby establishing him as the successor to the former rulers of the Roman Empire.

Because of the great distances involved in administering the kingdom, many areas were only symbolically under control of Charlemagne. Strong Germanic tribes, such as the Saxons, still wielded local power. As a result, the empire began to dissolve at the death of Charlemagne in 814 A.D. During the reign of Charlemagne's son, Louis the Pious, the local leaders began to strengthen their personal estates, and areas farther from the center of the kingdom began to grow exceedingly weaker.

In 843 A.D., Louis' sons signed the Treaty of Verdun which divided the empire into three parts. Louis received the territory of the East Franks that roughly corresponds with modern Germany. Charles laid claim to the territory of the West Franks that is roughly associated with the boundaries of modern France. The third son, Lothar, was named emperor and received land between the other two territories. This included lands extending from Belgium in the north to Italy in the south. Within years of the death of the Middle Franks' leader, this area was divided between the East and West Franks.

RISE OF SAXON RULE

Because of the control exerted by local leaders, the period from 919 to 1024 in German history was marked by militarily strong rulers. By the time the last leader of the Carolingians died at the beginning of the tenth century, five strong duchies had risen to power. These duchies were Franconia, Saxony, Swabia, Bayern, and Lothringen.

With the exception of Lothringen, the duchies united to elect a king. The second ruler, and first of the Saxon Dynasty, was Henry of Saxony who was elected in 919 A.D. He added Lothringen to his holdings and began to establish control over the local dukes. Henry's son Otto centralized control of the government by combining many of its functions with that of the church. This strengthened the control of the government, but also caused conflicts with the dukes, thereby setting the stage for future troubles.

Otto continued to expand his empire to include the eastern areas inhabited by the Slavs, Bohemians, and Poles and extended it south into Italy. In 962 A.D., the pope crowned Otto emperor of the Holy Roman Empire. As the emperors turned their attention to focusing and increasing the power of the empire, as well as expanding its borders, the local dukes again began to assert their power.

RISE OF THE SALIANS AND HOHENSTAUFFENS

When the last Saxon king died in 1024, control of the empire was transferred to the Salians by agreement among the major estate holders in the empire. The Salian kings strengthened the alliance of the church with the crown, which further angered the aristocratic leaders who suffered an additional loss of control. A long period of strife was initiated in 1077 when Pope Gregory VII insisted that Henry IV relinquish control of the German church. Seeing this as a way to strengthen their power, the local dukes allied themselves with the papacy. This period of discord led to the general weakening of the crown, including civil wars and loss of control over local leaders.

The year 1138 saw the rise of the first Hohenstauffen emperor. The second ruler, Frederick I or Frederick Barbarossa, restored some order to the empire. Under his policies, the various leaders in the free cities, principalities, and territories were again brought under one leader, although they retained local administration of each area and were not united as an empire. Some estimates place the number of principalities, territories, and free cities as high as 1,800. This territorial view led to many civil wars and attacks by invaders in the ensuing centuries, but it also contributed to the social and economic advance of the period.

RISE OF THE HAPSBURGS

The first of the Hapsburg rulers, Rudolph, came to power in 1273. Although the unity of the empire continued to deteriorate over following centuries, the empire saw great advances during this period. The first German universities were established in Prague, Cologne, Erfurt, Heidelberg, and Vienna. About 1350, the Hanse or Hanseatic League was created, linking towns for the benefit and protection of commerce. This action in turn lead to the creation of guilds to regulate craftsmen.

Germanic settlers also continued to expand to the east. The conquests of the Teutonic Knights provide an example of the large areas that were settled at this time. A religious order, the Teutonic Knights conquered areas in East Prussia. This allowed for an influx of settlers and helped establish cities in the Baltic region. Some of these cities were later incorporated as members of the Hanse.

At the end of the fifteenth century the Hapsburg Dynasty was in control of the largest part of Europe and was considered the sole world power. However, because its focus was on the dynasty base in Vienna, policies imposed were not thought of in terms of their benefit to the empire as a whole. Consequently, territorial princes continued to gain control and overtook many of the cities formerly associated with the Hanse. Of the more than seventy Germanic cities in existence at the time, only Lhbeck, Hamburg, and Bremen remained members of the Hanse at the end of the century.

The Reformation

Conflict among the various regions continued to build, and by the early sixteenth century, Germany was ripe for rebellion. The revolutionary catalyst was introduced in the form of Martin Luther in 1517 when he nailed his famous ninety-five theses to the door of the church at Wittenberg. Among Luther's teachings, which were circulated in pamphlets in 1520, was a call to the German princes to destroy papal power. Although this instilled in the peasants a vision of freedom from their landlords, it contrasted with Luther's teachings that laws, even if unjust, should be obeyed. In 1521, Charles V ordered Martin Luther to recant his teachings, but he refused and was given sanctuary by Frederick the Wise of Saxony. As a result of Luther's teachings, the Peasant War of 1524 was begun, but the king quickly put it down.

The reform movement continued to grow throughout the empire, and an attempt was made to reform it legally in 1555. The Augsburg Religious Peace dictated that the subjects of each prince would practice the prince's religion. Religious dissension did not end but was further fueled by a Counter Reformation led by the Jesuits. This movement was very successful in parts of Germany. One positive result of this movement was the mandate given in 1563 by the Catholic church to maintain marriage and christening records. The recording of deaths and other events followed at a later date. The Protestant churches also began to record vital records during this time.

During a short period of peace, the various groups began to unite. The seventeenth century saw the rise of the Bavarian Catholic League and the Palatinate Protestant Union. When the prince of Bohemia tried to reinstate Catholicism as the regional religion, armed conflict resulted. Austria-Spain, under the Hapsburg rule, combined with the Catholic League to combat the Protestant Union. Denmark, France, and Sweden aided the Protestants through their own desire to extend their power in Germany and thereby decrease the power of the Hapsburgs.

The ensuing Thirty Years War, lasting from 1618 to 1648, proved devastating to the country. Actually a series of wars rather than one long conflict, most of the battles were fought within Germanic borders and destroyed many towns and villages. It is estimated that one-third of the population, or approximately 7 million people were killed in the ensuing conflicts. Many Catholic and Protestant churches were destroyed, including their records.

Although the emperor still ruled, his power had been greatly reduced and the country was again reduced to a collection of principalities. The weakened state of the empire resulted in the loss of Pommerania, Elsaß-Lothringen (Alsace-Lorraine), Switzerland, and the Netherlands through military defeat and conquest.

Although the Thirty Years War diluted the power of many German states, the following years saw the rise in strength of the German state of Brandenburg under the rule of the Hollenzollerns. Led by Frederick Wilhelm, known as the Great Elector, Brandenburg began to expand its territories beginning in 1640. Its eastward expansion included reclaiming portions of Pommerania, which had been previously occupied by Sweden.

ℱORMATION OF THE ℘RUSSIAN ℰMPIRE

In 1701, Frederick Wilhelm's son, Frederick I, took the title King of Prussia. His son, Frederick Wilhelm I, focused his attention on building a strong well-maintained army. The largest percentage of the state budget went to maintaining these troops, which peaked at more than eighty-thousand soldiers. This focus placed a tremendous burden on the lower and middle class citizens who paid the majority of the taxes.

Under the continuing leadership of Frederick the Great, Prussia continued to expand into northeastern Europe. As this expansion continued, the Hapsburg empire, with its power base centralized in Austria, focused its attention on areas in southeastern Germany where it could withstand attacks by Turkish invaders.

When the last Hapsburg emperor died in 1742, he left only a female heir, Maria Theresa. Prussia took advantage of this opportunity to take control of Silesia, which was then under Austrian rule. The remaining German electors chose as their king Albert of Bavaria. Maria Theresa restructured the Hapsburg holdings and raised a massive army. In the Seven Years War, 1756 to 1763, Prussia defended its holdings and gained some additional land.

In 1772, Prussia and Austria both received territory with the division of Poland. This added West Prussia to the

Prussian lands. With the exception of areas occupied by the two large powers, Prussia and Austria, most Germanic regions lay under local control.

FRENCH RULE

Although Prussia proved to be a strong defender of its interests under Frederick's rule, its successive leaders were much weaker. This weakness became particularly crucial at the close of the eighteenth century with the beginning of the French Revolution in 1789. By 1792, France had turned its attention to lands occupied by Prussia and Austria. Prussia's initial response, aided by Austrian troops, was to invade France. Prussia's subsequent defeat and failure to regroup set the stage for Napoleon's advance in the following years.

Prussia's attention then was focused on its eastern borders where lands were gained in two subsequent partitions of Poland. In 1793, the French army moved against the lands along the Rhine. Prussia's withdrawal of its troops to avoid conflict served to strengthen Napoleon's strategy of dividing Prussia and Austria. When Austrian troops were defeated by French forces in 1800, the Russian and Prussian armies retreated. One positive result of this conquest was the beginning of civil registration of births, marriages, and deaths in 1798. (However, these were discontinued after the loss of French influence and did not start again until 1876.)

In 1805, Austrian forces suffered a major defeat at Austerlitz, along with Russian forces. This forced the dissolution of the Holy Roman Empire the following year. The French army made incursions on Prussian territory where garrisons were maintained through the French attack on Russia in 1812.

ᵀHE ᶜONFEDERATION OF THE ᴿHINE

In the years following the invasion of the Rhine, the various German principalities were divided among the states that had supported Napoleon. Combined under the Confederation of the Rhine, this area-encompassing areas outside the Prussian and Austrian borders and stretching as far as Hannover, Mecklenburg, and Saxony and including the new state of Westfalen-was protected by France. Positive effects of the French influence included centralized government as well as greater personal and religious rights.

The defeat of Napoleon's troops in Russia in 1812 and his subsequent withdrawal westward began the collapse of the Confederation of the Rhine. By promising to honor the territories established, Prussia was able to rally these German states and ally their troops with Russia and England. Napoleon was defeated in 1814 and finally at Waterloo in 1815.

A result of the Congress of Vienna was the restoration of some lands to Prussia. These included part of Saxony, a portion of Pommerania and the newly created states of Westfalen and Rhineland. The beginning of the nineteenth century marked a period of nationalism as reform swept the country, but the movement was slow to receive widespread support.

ᵀHE ᴳERMANIC ᶜONFEDERATION

The German territory became a hybrid of the future nation state and the former conglomeration of principalities, duchies, kingdoms, and free cities. Organized as the Germanic Confederation, it was a collection of thirty-nine states, each of which retained its own sovereignty and which was dominated by Austria. By 1820, five of these states had been granted constitutions. These included Bavaria, Baden,

Wüerttemberg, Saxe-Weimar, and the Duchy of Nassau.

The 1840s saw additional changes throughout the German territory. Many of the original thirty-nine states ceased to exist and were adopted into Prussia. In May 1848, the German Diet met with representatives of each state in the Confederation. A constitution was adopted in the form of the Declaration of Fundamental Rights. Reformists also sought to exclude Austria from a unified Germany and to establish the King of Prussia as the head of government. Ultimately, the Prussian King, Frederick Wilhelm IV, refused to reign without the full support of each area. Austria sought to quell this uprising militarily. Although the revolution failed as a whole, many of the ideas that had been presented became the basis for the coming years of German history.

The 1850s saw the rise of Otto von Bismarck as he came to power as the chief minister of Prussia. His efforts to strengthen the Prussian military position were widely opposed, although he received greater support in the mid-1860s. In 1864 a Prussian-Austrian alliance was created to halt Denmark's inroads to greater control of Schleswig-Holstein. The two Danish territories were quickly seized and divided. Prussia was given control of Schleswig and Austria of Holstein. Conflict with this dual control led Otto von Bismark to declare war on Austria in 1866. Austria's defeat within one month led to the Treaty of Prague and the demise of the German Confederation.

ESTABLISHMENT OF THE GERMAN EMPIRE

In 1867, the North German Confederation was established with a Prussian presidency. Ongoing conflict with France led to a declaration of war in 1870. This led to military alliances with the southern German states of Baden, Hesse-Darmstadt, Wüerttemberg, and Hesse-Darmstadt. By January

1871, decisive victories resulted in the addition of Alsace and portions of Lorraine to the newly created German Empire. Full power rested with the emperor, or Kaiser, through full veto power; however, but each state participated in enacting legislation. The reforms that swept the country fostered growth in industry, education, and commerce. In 1876, civil registration was established throughout the German Empire.

Although Otto von Bismarck had ultimately united Germany, he was forced from power as chancellor in 1890 over differing ideological views with Kaiser William II. Under William II's guidance, Germany set out to establish itself as a world power at the cost of diplomacy with surrounding nations. The exception was an alliance with Austria-Hungary and Italy.

The Rise of Modern Germany

In 1914 when a Serb assassinated the Austria-Hungary heir to the throne, Germany sided with Austria-Hungary in their declaration of war on Serbia. War with Russia quickly followed and brought Germany into conflict with an alliance between Serbia, Russia, France, Britain, Italy in 1915, and the United States in 1917. German forces were ultimately driven back from the areas of western invasion in 1918. This act ultimately led to Germany's surrender and the breakdown of the German government. Under the terms of the peace treaty in 1919, Germany lost major portions of its former empire. The largest sections were the loss of West Prussia to Poland, and loss of the majority of Posen and part of Schleswig.

Following the peace treaty, a new republic, known as the Weimar Republic, was established as the new democratic form of government in Germany. During the following years, the new republic struggled with economic depression, resulting in its efforts to rebuild the country following the war. In the

1930s, the radical Nazi party took advantage of this opportunity to attract support to their vision of saving the country. Under the leadership of Adolph Hitler, who was named chancellor and ultimately dictator in 1934, Germany again began to build its armies. In 1936, Germany formed alliances with Japan and Italy. Hitler set out to retake those territories that had been lost at the close of World War I. In 1938, Germany invaded Austria and later Czechoslovakia.

Germany's invasion of Poland brought about a declaration of war from France and England, but the declaration failed to stop the German troops who continued their invasion of Europe. This led to the occupation by German forces of Denmark, Norway, Belgium, the Netherlands, portions of France, and areas of eastern Europe. Military objectives extended Germany's reach to include areas in Africa.

Germany invaded the Soviet Union in 1941, but was defeated by early 1943. The year 1941 also saw the entry of the United States into the war. After the defeat of the German army in Russia, an alliance comprising the United States, France, Britain, and Russia forced back the German forces. In 1945, with the opposing forces approaching Berlin, Germany surrendered.

The terms of the peace treaty again brought about loss of former German territories. Most of the eastern areas were given to Poland, with part of East Prussia going to the Soviet Union. The remaining portions of Germany were divided in fourths among the allies with the United States, France, Britain, and the Soviet Union each taking control of one part. Each country also controlled part of the city of Berlin.

In 1949, Germany was redivided and two separate countries were established-the Federal Republic of Germany, better known as West Germany, and the German Democratic Republic, which was known as East Germany. The German Democratic Republic remained officially under the control of the Soviet Union until 1955, but unofficially, this association continued much later. In 1961, the Berlin Wall was erected to stem the flood of citizens seeking to flee the German Democratic Republic due to the poor conditions in the country.

While the German Democratic Republic struggled under Communist control, the Federal Republic of Germany flourished as an independent country after 1955 when final control by the allies was withdrawn. Beginning in 1973, when a treaty was signed between them, East and West Germany continued to strengthen their relations. In November 1989, the Berlin Wall was brought down again, allowing free movement between the two countries. They were officially united as the Bundesrepulik Deutschland on 3 October 1990.

GERMAN EMIGRATION

In reviewing the history of the country known today as Germany, researchers find many reasons why their ancestors might have left Germany. German immigrants first tried to settle in the Americas in 1562, but they did not create a permanent settlement until 1683 when they settled Germantown in Philadelphia.

During the 1700s, individuals left Germany for several reasons. As previously discussed, religious persecution forced many people to leave their homes and seek settlement elsewhere. Not only were religious persecutions severe, but the effects of the Thirty Years War devastated the countryside. For those reasons, combined with the despotic rule of the German leaders, it is no wonder that conditions elsewhere seemed so enticing. Many immigrants during this period, known as Palatines, came from the southern regions of Germany.

German emigration to the United States continued throughout the nineteenth century. Circumstances in their homeland forced many Germans to consider such a drastic move. The influx of Germans into the United States continued through the beginning of the twentieth century when it finally began to decline. Reasons for the influx included a famine in the 1840s and the lack of available land to settle in Germany. As land became more available in the United States and the wars of the Prussian army pressured the citizens, the number of immigrants sharply increased.

More German immigrants arrived in the United States during this time than any other nationality. Consequently, there are millions of people of German descent who remain in the dark about their German heritage because their families have not been traced prior to the twentieth century. Researchers who have traced their ancestry to an immigrant ancestor have an exciting opportunity to learn about the way their ancestors lived through this rapidly changing period of history.

SUMMARY

An understanding of the continual historical conflict, which beset the area we know today as Germany, establishes a solid base for a German researcher to begin work. Germany did not attain cohesion as a nation until the latter nineteenth century, much later than the time period with which most researchers are probably working. Knowing the history of a region often provides the reason an ancestor moved from a given area or why records are not available for certain periods. Additionally, an understanding of the strength of the principalities, kingdoms, duchies, and free states allows researchers to achieve greater success by focusing their attention on these regional records. The types of records available and their current locations are discussed in later chapters.

CHAPTER TWO

RESEARCH TOOLS AND TIPS

RESEARCH TOOLS

Most researchers have established research procedures to fit their particular research style, and all researchers find specific tools to help them to achieve their individual research goals. Because German research can involve many boundary and jurisdictional changes, not to mention a foreign language, several tools, perhaps not required in previous research, are essential to success in researching your family. These tools include gazetteers, maps, dictionaries for the areas you are researching, and online sources.

GAZETTEERS

A good gazetteer is one of the most essential tools for conducting German research. Because of the many boundary changes, it is important not only to identify the locality in which your ancestor previously resided, but also to know where the town is currently located. In addition, a gazetteer can assist in identifying a specific church parish if the town in which your ancestor resided did not have its own church. Similarly, it is necessary to identify the civil registration office when seeking civil records of births, marriages, and deaths once recording of them began, however, most regions did not begin to maintain these types of records until they were required in 1876.

Among the best gazetteers available is Meyers Orts- und Verkehrslexikon des Deutschen Reiches, ed. E. Uetrecht, 1912 edition. This gazetteer identifies towns with present locations outside the area of modern Germany. Copies of this source can be viewed on microfiche at a family history center of The Church of Jesus Christ of Latter-day Saints.

GEOserv is a service available on the Internet that can help you identify the location of towns in modern day Germany. This service, established by Arthur Teschler, responds to e-mail queries. The return e-mail identifies the town by its current name, the county in which it is located, the its Regierungsbezirk (administrative unit), the German state it is located in, the current postal code, the population as of 1989, and the latitude and longitude. Originally established prior to the reunification of Germany, some of the records for areas formerly in East Germany are not included but will be added at a future date. Full instructions on using GEOserv and an explanation of its limitations are located at <http://www.genealogy.com/gene/www/abt/geoserv.html>.

For the modern locations of place-names outside the United States, visit the GEOnet Names Server at <http://www.nima.mil/gns/html/index.html>.

MAPS

Another commonly overlooked resource is a map detailed enough to show the location of the ancestral town you are researching. This allows for closer differentiation of boundaries and the ability to determine precisley how cloe to a given border a town is situated. This can aid in identifying new research strategies or suggest additional records that should be searched. In addition, if it is necessary to conduct a radius search of surrounding parishes, a detailed map is essential to ensure that you search appropriate areas and to help you identify towns near your ancestor's place of residence.

ᴅICTIONARIES

Because the records you research are recorded in their original language (German, Latin, Polish, etc.), a good dictionary is imperative to help you accurately translate information from the original records.

Since the records are often decades or even hundreds of years old, many terms in common use at the time an ancestor was living are no longer found in the modern language. Even researchers with a good grasp of the modern language find a dictionary listing archaic occupations and causes of death to be essential.

Several German/English dictionaries are on the Internet at <http://dictionaries.travlang.com/German English/> and <http://www.gmsmuc.de/look.html>.

References to archaic occupations and causes of death are located at <http://www.germanscript.com/reference.htm>.

ᴏNLINE ʀESEARCH ᴛOOLS

Recent and rapid advances in computer technology have made resources available that only a few years ago were impossible to produce. A beginning researcher now has much greater potential for obtaining results; however, researchers who ignore these advances make their research more difficult.

Among the computer capabilities most advantageous to genealogists is the ability to store large quantities of data on CD-ROM. This medium has allowed the extraction and publishing of research tools, and in some cases, actual sources of genealogical data. You can have at your fingertips the necessary gazetteers, maps, dictionaries, and directories while traveling to various research localities.

ℰLECTRONIC ℛECORDS

Many products have been introduced that record data in different electronic formats. These programs or applications are available for different computers. Users of PCs using DOS, Windows, or Macintosh OS can record data in an easy-to-use formats and readily exchange their information with other researchers via e-mail, floppy disk, Zip disk or, increasingly, CD-ROM.

One of the main advantages to computerized information is the ability to share it with others. By sharing with other researchers, you can better utilize your time and effort by avoiding duplication of research on lines that have already been examined by someone else.

Another advantage is that you do not have to re-record family history data received from someone else. New information can be exchanged electronically via GEDCOM file, an exchange format unique to genealogy applications. Once connected, new data is immediately displayed on the computer, and updated pedigree charts and family group sheets can be printed showing the new information. You can cite sources and record full transcriptions without transporting heavy printed records from one research locality to another with the ease and convenience of an e-mail message or other transmission method.

ℭHE ℑNTERNET

Over the last few years, the Internet has grown at breathtaking speed. Using the Internet, you can easily correspond with relatives in foreign countries, access research tools as you need them, and search sources, such as extracted parish records, which are being posted daily on the Internet.

The Internet has put many reference aids at your fingertips. In addition to the reference aids cited earlier, some Internet sites are devoted to specific types of research. These locations on the Internet can help you learn research techniques, provide information on record locations and new sources, and let you contact other researchers who are researching the same surnames or areas.

Many sites for German research are available, although two provide a "springboard" for new researchers. Not only do they provide sources for German researchers, but they have links to sites that teach new users how to better utlilize the Internet and find the information they seek. These sites can be found on the Web at <http://www.Cyndislist.com> and <http://www.worldgenweb.org>.

You can, in some instances, contact German archives to determine the records they have, hours of operation, fees, and whether they conduct research through correspondence. This preparatory contact can save the disappointment of waiting weeks for an anticipated result by mail only to find that the desired records are located elsewhere.

ℙOTENTIAL ℙITFALLS

Even when you use the best tools and techniques, you may be frustrated with German research by such things as inconsistent spelling of surnames and place-names, naming convention idiosyncrasies, and finding the current locations of records. Knowing in advance what to expect will help you be more accurate and efficient in your research.

Spelling Errors

Perhaps the greatest potential problem when beginning research in Germany is the spelling of surnames and locality names as they were taken from family sources or original United States sources. Frustration is likely if you do not know that a large percentage of the populations, including many of our ancestors, were illiterate prior to the twentieth century. Consequently, the spelling of surnames and location names often reflects the way they sounded to the record keeper. In German, as in English, the substitution of vowels is among the most common errors, particularly when an umlaut is substituted for another vowel.

When trying to identify locations, bear in mind that a particular ancestor may have spoken with a regional dialect, thereby giving the name of a locality a much different inflection than would normally be heard. Awareness of the potential for these types of errors can aid you in identifying an ancestral residence or in identifying a given ancestor in an original written record. This will allow the consideration of a broad range of possible spellings.

Even when researching in written German records, spelling variations sometimes prove challenging. As you research backward through the records, phonetic variants of a surname often appear. It is also common to find variant spellings if your ancestor moved from one parish to another. Bearing in mind possible spelling variants of surnames or locality names ensures that you read and evaluate all pertinent records.

ꓘAMING ꓑRACTICES

Naming practices in various Germanic regions also can sometimes prove frustrating for new researchers. These conventions may include patronymics, abbreviations, nicknames, pet names, and multiple given names.

If you are researching in the Schleswig-Holstein or Ostfriesland regions, you may be surprised to find the use of patronymics. This practice of deriving a surname from the given name of the father is more commonly found in Scandinavian countries. By acquainting yourself with the records of a given locality you can ensure that you trace the correct lineage rather than an erroneous one through misinterpretation of written sources.

Other practices common throughout many areas of Germany include the use of abbreviations in written entries and the use of nicknames for parents and children. The birth of a child, Maria Klein, might be recorded as M. Klein, or Johannes Schmidt may appear in the records under the nickname of Hans.

The use of multiple given names was also a common practice throughout much of Germany. In some instances, the recording of a given name may appear only on a christening record and not on records created later in a person's life.

These are by no means the only types of naming practices used throughout Germany, although they are among the most common. Knowing that such practices were used during some time periods and in some localities, it is wise to acquaint yourself with the history of the region and the practices that were used during the time of your ancestors' residence.

DATE PROBLEMS

Over the course of German history, various areas have utilized different types of calendars. Prior to 1582, most regions used the Julian calendar, but it was later replaced with the Gregorian calendar, which resulted in an adjustment of ten days to make up for discrepancies over the years. Because Catholic regions were among the few areas that adopted the calendar when it was first introduced, dating practices vary depending on when a particular area made the change. Again, it is wise to become acquainted with the local history of an area.

In addition to the change made to the regular calendar, the French Revolutionary Calendar was introduced in regions brought under the rule of France. Published charts are available to convert the dates on this calendar to the corresponding dates on the Gregorian calendar.

Parishes used a third form of dating, regarding religious holidays. Because these feast days were based on the seasons, some of them were fixed on specific days and others adjusted dates with the seasons. An example of the moveable type of feast day would be Easter, which does not fall on the same date each year. It is common to find early records referenced by the feast day they occurred on rather than by the actual date. Consult a published chart to convert the dates obtained from parish registers to dates you can use in your records.

CURRENT LOCATIONS OF RECORDS

As previously discussed, success in researching German ancestors depends on identifying specific localities and perusing the records for those areas. Even when you know a locality, accessing the records for a given area can be challenging because of Germany's volatile history. Due to territorial disputes, wars, and boundary changes, regions formerly associated with the area we know as Germany may now be located within the jurisdiction of another German state, or perhaps another country.

The following list does not comprise detailed boundary divisions, but it does provide an overview of the current locations of former territories. In each instance a duchy, kingdom, principality, etc., is listed by its designation in 1871, along with any subdivisions. These are followed by the current German state or foreign country location.

Place	1871 Designation	Subdivision	Current Area
ANHALT	Anhalt-Bernburg Anhalt-Dessau Anhalt-Köthen		
SACHSEN-ANHALT			
BADEN			
BADEN-WÜRTTEMBERG			
BAYERN	Niederbayern Oberbayern Mittelfranken Unterfranken Oberfranken Oberpfalz Rheinpfalz Schwaben	Bayern Bayern Bayern Bayern Bayern Bayern Rheinland-Pfalz Bayern	
BRAUNSCHWEIG			
NIEDERSACHSEN			
ELSAß-LOTHRINGEN			
FRANCE			
HESSEN	Hessen-Darmstadt Hessen-Homburg Hesse-Kassel	Hessen Rheinland-Pfalz Hessen Hessen	
LIPPE			
NORDRHEIN-WESTFALEN			
MECKLENBERG	Mecklenburg-Schwerin Mecklenburg-Strelitz	Mecklenburg Mecklenburg	Vorpommern Vorpommern
NASSAU			
HESSEN			
OLDENBURG (GRAND DUCHY)	Birkenfeld Lübeck Oldenburg (Duchy)	Rheinland-Pfalz Schleswig-Holstein Niedersachen	Saarland

Place (cont'd)	1871 Designation	Subdivision	Current Area
PRUSSIA *(KINGDOM)*	Brandenburg Hannover (kingdom) Hessen-Nassau Hohenzollern Ostpreussen Pommern Posen Rheinprovinz Sachsen (province) Silesia Westfalen	Brenadenburg/Poland Niedersachen Hessen Baden-Württemberg Russia/Lithuania/Poland Mecklenburg Poland Nordrhein-Westfalen Rheinland-Pfalz/ Belgium Sachsen-Anhalt/ Thüringen Sachsen/Poland Nordrhein-Westfalen	Vorpommen/Poland
SACHSEN *(KINGDOM)*			
SACHSEN			
SCHAUMBERG- *LIPPE*			
NIEDERSACHSEN			
SCHLESWIG- *HOLSTEIN &* *LOWENSTEIN*	Holstein Lauenburg Schleswig	Schleswig-Holstein Schleswig-Holstein Schleswig-Holstein/ Denmark	
THÜRINGEN			
THÜRINGEN			
WALDECK			
HESSEN			
WÜRTTEMBERG			
BADEN- *WÜRTTEMBERG*			

CHAPTER THREE

GERMAN GENEALOGICAL SOURCES

IVIL REGISTRATION RECORDS did not exist for most areas where German ancestors may have resided prior to the mid-1870s. Thus, church parish registers are among the primary sources used for beginning research in Germany. Many families cannot be traced earlier than the parish registers because of a lack of available records for the family. Other sources may allow further extension of the lineage; however, researchers are often unacquainted with the available sources or they become discouraged by their seeming inaccessibility. The following sections discuss some of the sources that may offer further potential in tracing your ancestral lineage.

CHURCH RECORDS (KIRCHENBÜCHER)

As mentioned above, church records are among the first sources used by the beginning researcher. To access church records, you must first identify the parish to which your ancestors may have belonged. By utilizing a gazetteer as previously discussed, you can find the locality in which your ancestors resided and the parish church they attended. If you know your ancestors' religion, you will save time spent searching unnecessary sources.

Once you have identified the parish church you can examine the church records themselves. Several different types of records can be found within church registers. As a rule, the more recent the records, the more information they contain. These records include, but are not limited to, the following sources.

ƑAMILY ʀEGISTERS (ƑAMILIENREGISTER)

Family registers are found throughout Germany but are more frequently found in the southern localities. These registers may be located in various archives and civil depositories but are often associated with a church parish. These handwritten records usually record the entire family, listing the names, dates of birth and death of each individual, and the marriage date of the parents. In some instances, the names of the mother's and father's parents are also given. It is not unusual to find entries referencing a move to another locality or perhaps to another country. Instances of the phrase, "nach Amerika," can aid in confirming that you have located the correct family. Although many of these registers extend only to the early 1800s, many extend into the eighteenth century or, in some cases, to the beginning of the parish.

ßAPTISMAL ʀEGISTERS (ɢAUFREGISTER)

Some parishes used a birth register (Gerburtsregister) instead of a baptismal register. At a minimum, these registers usually contain the date of baptism or birth, the name of the child, the name of the father, and the names of the witnesses. Other information, depending on the particular register and the time period, may include the father's residence and occu-

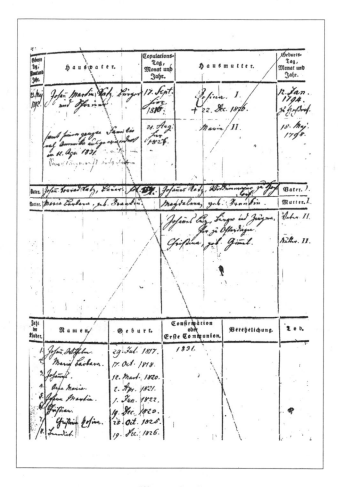

Illustration 1
Familienregister, Remmingsheim, Württemberg, Germany

This example of a family register contains information on each family member regarding their name, birthdate and place, confirmation, marriage, and death. In this particular record the specific information was recorded that the family left for America on April 13, 1831.

pation, the name of the mother, and the child's date of death or burial if the child died young.

CONFIRMATION REGISTERS (KONFIRMATIONREGISTER)

Confirmation registers contain the name of the confirmed and the date of confirmation. Other information may include the name and occupation of the father, the name of the mother, and the date and birthplace of the confirmed. In most instances, confirmation occurred between the ages of twelve and fourteen, although it could occur either earlier or later depending on the locality. Confirmation registers can often be used to track a family that moved into a parish after the births but before the confirmations of their children.

MARRIAGE REGISTERS (TRAUREGISTER)

At the very least, marriage registers contain the name of the bride and groom and the date of marriage. Additional information may include the residence of the participants; the names, residences, and occupations of their fathers; the names of their mothers; the birth dates and birthplaces of the bride and groom, and often, if it was a first or subsequent marriage.

DEATH REGISTERS (STERBEREGISTER)

Death or burial (Grabenregister) records provide the name of the deceased and the date of death or burial. Often, the age of the deceased is given. Additional information may include the cause of death, the location of death, the maiden name of a deceased woman, or the names of the parents of the deceased. The name of the surviving spouse is often given and, in rare instances, the names of surviving children.

CENSUS RECORDS (Volkszählungen)

Because of the fragmented nature of historic Germany, and unlike federal census records of the United States, any type of census was taken on a regional basis rather than for Germany as a unified country. Only a few areas took censuses on a regular basis, although scattered census records can be found in other regions of Germany. Schleswig-Holstein,

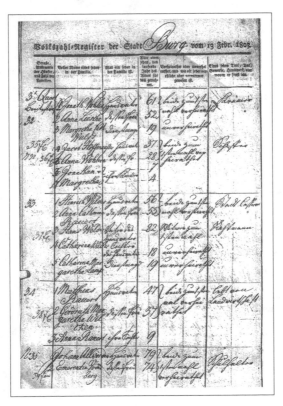

Illustration 2
1803 Schleswig-Holstein Census

This census record, taken in the parish of Burg on the Isle of Fehmarn, records the name of each member of the household, their relationship to the head of the house, their age, and their occupation.

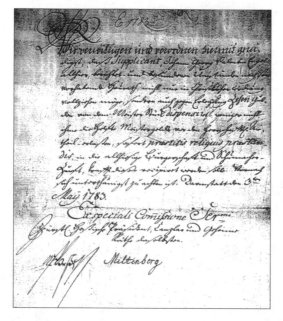

**Illustration 3
1783 Bürgerbuch,
Darmstadt, Hessen,
Germany**

This entry records the arrival of Johann Georg Valentin Engel in Darmstadt and his application for citizenship in the city.

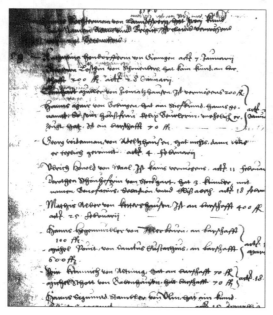

**Illustration 4
Bürgerbuch,
Augsburg, Bayern,
Germany, 1558**

Although this record does not contain the specific information shown in the previous example, it does serve as a census substitute for the town by showing all of the male citizens in the city.

Mecklenburg, and Württemberg are among the locations with good census records.

Although not true census records, citizen rolls (bürgerlisten) for a particular city can serve as a census substitute. They can be particularly helpful in determining when your ancestor arrived in a town from another area.

Vital Records

Civil registration of births, marriages, and deaths was required after 1876. Some areas began keeping records as early as the late 1700s or early 1800s due to occupation by Napoleon's forces. The information contained in a civil registration is similar to that contained in parish registers, although the events are always marriages, births, and deaths rather than baptisms and burials.

Often, civil registration records are easier to use than parish registers because printed forms were used at the later dates and indexes were introduced. Also, it is not necessary to know the religion of an ancestor because civil registration records recorded all of the city residents.

Civil registration records often contain more information than corresponding parish registers, although the parish registers are more likely to contain extraneous information, such as a detailed account of an unusual death. This is because the parish authorities were likely to be closely acquainted with an individual family.

Emigration Sources

Emigration sources are located in various local German archives. The locations of some archives are given in chapter 5. Emigration sources can include, but are not limited to, emigration lists (auswanderunglisten), resident registrations lists

**Illustration 5
Württemberg
Emigration Permit,
1866**

In this example the
Auswanderungs–Paß
(emigration pass) pro-
vides a physical descrip-
tion of the applicant,
Emmerentzia Sauer.
It also tells us she trav-
eled to North America
through Baden, Hessen,
Hannover, and Bremen.

(einwohnermeldelisten), and passenger lists (passagierlisten
or shiffslisten). The auswanderungslisten can be particularly
helpful in obtaining information about an immigrant ancestor. Unfortunately, many individuals left Germany without
applying for permission to emigrate. If your ancestor moved
within Germany, local recording of internal migration began
in the early nineteenth century. The registration of a town's
residents (einwohnermeldelisten) recorded the movements of
families within the German Empire and are located at the
office of the local registrar.

OCCUPATIONAL SOURCES

Occupational records usually take the form of apprentice-
ship applications or records of guild lists. An individual had to
be a member of the local guild to practice a trade in a given

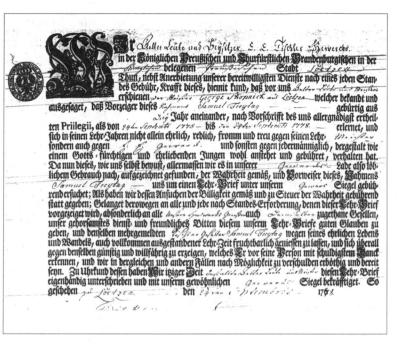

Illustration 6
Tischler (cabinetmaker) Guild Records,
Lötzen, East Prussia, Prussia, 1778

This record for Samuel Freytage documents his service in learning the cabinet-maker trade and allows him to practice his trade in the town.

town. The guild ensured that all practicing tradesmen were strong, upstanding citizens of the community. Although early guild records often comprise only a list of names of the members, even such scanty information can be used in lieu of a census, particularly when it predates the parish registers for the area.

Guild applications often contain very useful information about an individual. This may include a prior residence, the place and date of birth, the names of parents, and if applicable, the name of a spouse and any children. The person's date of arrival in the city is usually recorded along with a history of time spent as an apprentice or journeyman. These records are usually found in the local archives.

COURT RECORDS

Court records in Germany are similar to those you may have used previously in the United States. These records may include civil disputes and court trials as well as probate records. If your ancestor owned property, there may be a will or other testament record. These records are located in the various local and state archives.

LAND RECORDS

If the family you are researching owned property, recorded land transactions can often be used to trace a family much earlier than parish registers begin. Although many of the ancestors sought are tenant farmers, some acquired property. Deeds record the names of the grantor and grantee, their residences at the time, the date of the transaction, and the amount paid. In some cases, the information recorded by the city also includes information regarding heirs of the landholder.

MILITARY RECORDS

Military records can be very useful but may prove time consuming and difficult to locate because they are widely scattered throughout Germany. To access the majority of records, you must know the unit in which your ancestor served before a record can be located; therefore, use of these records is often a last resort. In instances where records are available showing registration for service, the birthplace of your migrant ancestor may be included.

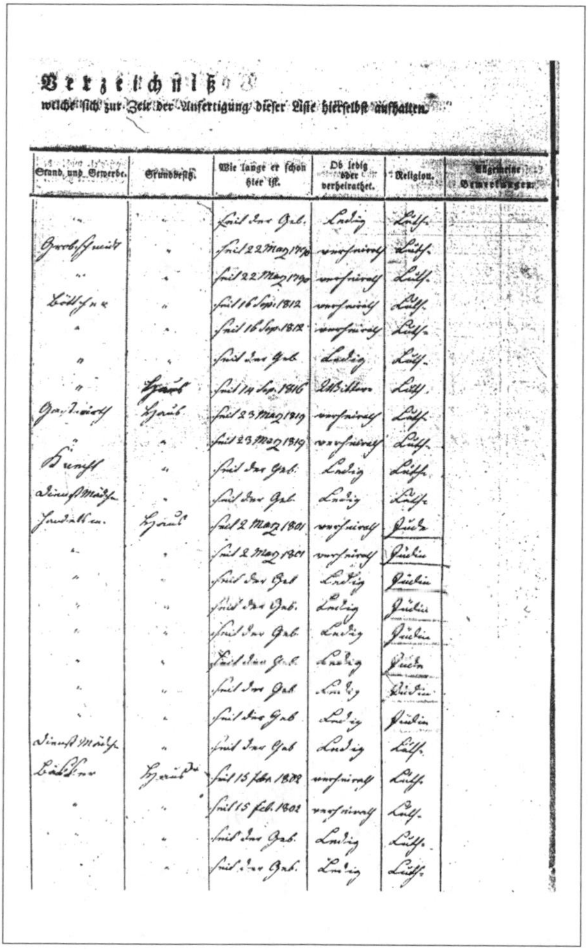

Verzeichniß
welche sich zur Zeit der Anfertigung dieser Liste hierselbst aufhalten.

Stand und Gewerbe.	Grundbesitz.	Wie lange er schon hier ist.	Ob ledig oder verheirathet.	Religion.	Allgemeine Bemerkungen.
"	"	seit der Geb.	Ledig	Luth.	
Grobschmidt	"	seit 22 May 1790	verheirath	Luth.	
"	"	seit 22 May 1790	verheirath	Luth.	
Böttcher	"	seit 16 Sept. 1812	verheirath	Luth.	
"	"	seit 16 Sept. 1812	verheirath	Luth.	
"	"	seit der Geb.	Ledig	Luth.	
"	Haus	seit 14 Sep. 1816	Wittwe	Luth.	
Gastwirth	Haus	seit 23 May 1819	verheirath	Luth.	
"	"	seit 23 May 1819	verheirath	Luth.	
Knecht	"	seit der Geb.	Ledig	Luth.	
Dienstmädchen	"	seit der Geb.	Ledig	Luth.	
Handelsm.	Haus	seit 2 May 1801	verheirath	Jude	
"	"	seit 2 May 1801	verheirath	Jüdin	
"	"	seit der Geb.	Ledig	Jüdin	
"	"	seit der Geb.	Ledig	Jüdin	
"	"	seit der Geb.	Ledig	Jüdin	
"	"	seit der Geb.	Ledig	Jude	
"	"	seit der Geb.	Ledig	Jüdin	
"	"	seit der Geb.	Ledig	Jüdin	
Dienstmädch.	"	seit der Geb.	Ledig	Luth.	
Bäcker	Haus	seit 15 Febr. 1802	verheirath	Luth.	
"	"	seit 15 Feb. 1802	verheirath	Luth.	
"	"	seit der Geb.	Ledig	Luth.	
"	"	seit der Geb.	Ledig	Luth.	

Illustration 7
Land Owners of Burg (auf Fehmarn), Schleswig, Holstein, Germany

This record records all of the property owners in the town. It provides much the same information which would be found in a census by showing the location of the property, the name of the owner, the names of the sons as well as the date of death for of those listed. In addition their age as of March 1, 1834 is recorded.

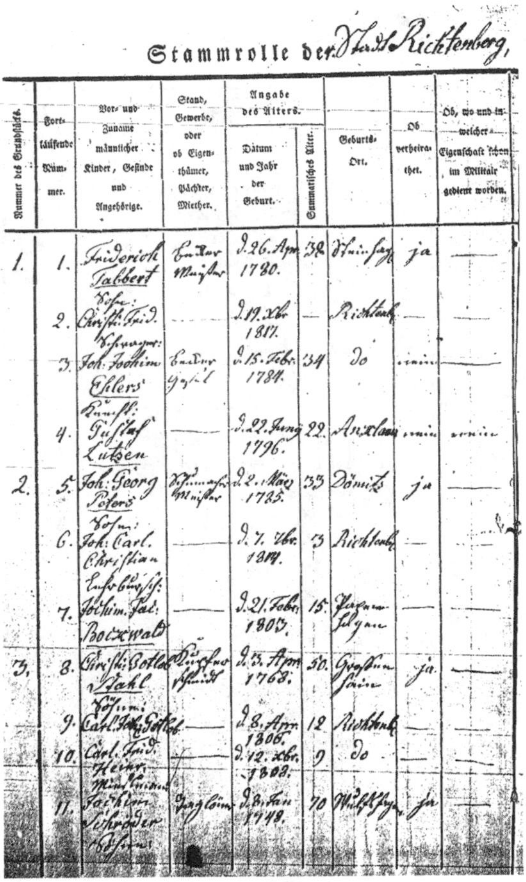

Stammrolle der Stadt Richtenberg,

Nummer des Grundstücks	Fortlaufende Nummer	Vor- und Zuname männlicher Kinder, Gesinde und Angehörige	Stand, Gewerbe, oder ob Eigenthümer, Pächter, Miether	Angabe des Alters: Datum und Jahr der Geburt	Angabe des Alters: Summarisches Alter	Geburts-Ort	Ob verheirathet	Ob, wo und in welcher Eigenschaft schon im Militair gedient worden
1.	1.	Friderich Talbert	[illegible] Meister	d. 26. Apr 1780.	38	[illegible]	ja	—
	2.	Sohn: Christ. Frid.		d. 19. Xbr 1817.	—	Richtenb.	—	—
	3.	Schwager: Joh. Jochim Ehlers	[illegible]	d. 15. Febr. 1784.	34	do	[illegible]	—
	4.	[illegible]: Gustaf Lutzen	—	d. 22. Aug 1796.	22	Anklam	[illegible]	[illegible]
2.	5.	Joh. Georg Peters	[illegible] Meister	d. 2. März 1785.	33	Dömitz	ja	—
	6.	Sohn: Joh. Carl. Christian	—	d. 7. 9br 1814.	3	Richtenb.	—	—
	7.	[illegible]: Jochim. Dal. Bockwald	—	d. 21. Febr 1803.	15.	[illegible]	—	—
3.	8.	Christ. Gottlob Stahl	[illegible] schmidt	d. 3. Apr 1768.	50.	[illegible]	ja.	—
	9.	Söhne: Carl. Joh. Gottlob	—	d. 8. Apr 1806.	12	Richtenb.	—	—
	10.	Carl. Frid. Heinr.	—	d. 12. Xbr. 1808.	9	do	—	—
	11.	[illegible]: Jochim Schröder	Tagelöhner	d. [illegible] Jan 1748.	70	[illegible]	ja	

Illustration 8
Stammrolle, Richtenburg, Pommern, Prussia

This record, on this and the following page, shows each male residents registration for military service records their name, any male children in their home, their occupation, birthdate and place, whether married, and details of previous military service.

ᒍISCELLANEOUS ᔕOURCES

Among the many additional types of sources that can be found in varying forms throughout Germany are citizen rolls, tax lists, newspapers, city chronicles, school records, address books, German lineage books, and published funeral sermons.

Another source that bears mentioning is the family book (Ortsippenbuch). These local family books comprise an accounting of all of the residents in a given area. Vital record events are recorded as taken from the parish registers. In some

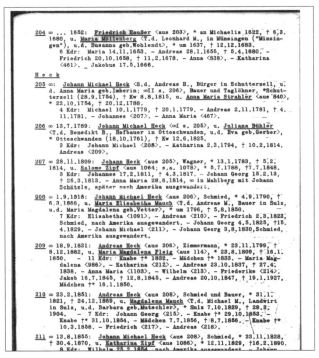

Illustration 9
Dorssippenbuch Kippenheimweiler, Baden, Germany

This example taken from an ortsippenbuch shows the quantity of information which can be found on each individual. Each surname is traced back in the parish until its first appearance.

instances, the information has been augmented with records from the local archives. These published sources are available in many libraries, and many of them are available on microfilm through the LDS Family History Library in Salt Lake City, Utah. When available, family books should not be overlooked.

The following chapters list several resources important to the German researcher. These include church archives, regional archives, and family organizations in Germany. It is in these repositories that you may find lesser used sources, which may enable you to extend your ancestry further than you have thought possible.

CHAPTER FOUR

CHURCH RECORDS

EVANGELICAL CHURCH IN GERMANY

Evangelical Church in Germany (Evangelische Kirche in Deutschland), also known by the acronym EKD, is composed of twenty-four regional churches. These are a compilation of Lutheran, Reformed, and United churches, which are governed by an elected Synod, Council, and Church Conference. The following list provides the name of the regional church, the location of the church archives, and its Internet address, if available.

Germany
Evangelisches Zentralarchiv in Berlin
Jebensstraße 3
D-10623 Berlin

Anhalt
Evangelische Landeskirche Anhalts
www.ekd.de/kirche/anhalte.html

Evangelische Landeskirche
Anhalts Landeskirchenamt
Landeskirchliches Archiv
Friedrichstraße 22
D-09844 Dessau

Baden
Evangelische Landeskirche in Baden
www.ekd.de/kirche/badene.html

Evangelische Landeskirche in Baden
Evangelische Oberkirchenrat
Landeskirchliches Archiv
Blumenstraße 1
D-76133 Karlsruhe

Bayern
Evangelisch-Lutherische Kirche in Bayern
www.epv.de

Evangelisch-Lutherische Kirche in Bayern
Landeskirchliches Archiv
Veilhofstraße 28
D-90489 Nürnberg

Berlin-Brandenburg
Evangelische Kirche in Berlin-Brandenburg
www.ekibb.com

Evangelische Kirche in Berlin-Brandenburg
Neue Grünstraße 19-22
D-10179 Berlin

Landeskirchliches Archiv und Konsistorium Berlin
Bachstraße 1
D-10555 Berlin

Braunschweig
Evangelisch-lutherische Landeskirche in Braunschweig
www.luth-braunschweig.de

Evangelisch-lutherische
Landeskirche in Braunschweig
Landskirchliches Archiv
Alter Zeughof 1
D-38100 Braunschweig

Bremen
Bremishe Evengelische Kirche
www.ekd.de/kirche/bremene.html

Bremische Evangelische Kirche
Landeskirchliches Archiv
Postfach 106929
D-27469 Bremen

Bremische Evangelische Kirche
Landeskirchliches Archiv
Franziuseck 2-4
D-28199 Bremen

Hannover
Evangelisch-Lutherische Landeskirche Hannovers
www.ev/ka.de/

Evangelisch-Lutherische
Landeskirche Hannovers
Landeskirchliches Archiv
Am Steinbruch 14
D-30449 Hannover

Hessen and Nassau

Evangelische Kirche in Hessen und Nassau
www.ekhn.de/

Evangelische Kirche in Hessen und Nassau
Zentralarchiv
Ahastraße 5a
D-64285 Darmstadt

Evangelische Kirche in Hessen und Nassau
Zentralarchiv
D-64285 Darmstadt

Kurhessen (Hesse-Kassel) and Waldeck

Evangelische Kirche von Kurhessen-Waldeck
www.ekkw.de

Evangelische Kirche von Kurhessen-Waldeck
Landeskirchliches Archiv
Lessingstraße 15a
D-34119 Kassel-Wilhelmshöhe

Lippe

Lippische Landeskirche
www.lippische.landeskirche.de

Lippische Landeskirche Archiv
Leopoldstraße 27
D-32756 Detmold

Mecklenburg

Evangelisch-Lutherische Landeskirche Mecklenburgs
www.ekd.de/kirche/mecklene.html

Evangelisch-Lutherische
Landeskirche Mecklenburgs
Landeskirchliches Archiv

Münzstraße 8
D-19010 Schwerin

Evangelisch-Lutherische
Landeskirche Mecklenburgs
Landeskirchliches Archiv
Postfach 011003
D-19010 Schwerin

Domarchiv Ratzeburg
Domhof 35
D-23909 Ratzeburg

Nordelb
Nordelbische Evangelisch-Lutherische Kirche
www.nordelbien.de

Nordelbische Evangelisch-Lutherische Kirche
Nordelbisches Kirchenarchiv Kiel
Dänische Straße 21–35
D-24103 Kiel

Oldenburg
Evangelisch-Lutherische Kirche in Oldenburg
www.home.t-online.de/home/
ev.kirche.oldenburg/homepage.htm

Evangelisch-Lutherische Kirche in Oldenburg
Archiv der Evangelisch-Lutherische Oberkirchenrates
Philosophenweg 1
D-26121 Oldenburg

Evangelisch-Luterhische Kirche in Oldenburg
Archiv der Evangelisch-Lutherische Oberkirchenrates
Postfach 1709
D-26007 Oldenburg

Pfalz
Evangelische Kirche der Pfalz
www.evpfalz.de

Evangelische Kirche der Pfalz
Zentralarchiv
Domplatz 6
D-67346 Speyer

Pommern
Pommersche Evangelische Kirche
www.ekd.de/kirche/pommerne.html

Pommersche Evangelische Kirche
Landeskirchliches Archiv
Karl-Marx-Platz 15
D-17489 Greifswald

Pommersche Evangelische Kirche
Landeskirchliches Archiv
Postfach 187
D-17461 Greifswald

Bayern (Reformed)
Evangelisch-Reformierten Kirche in Nordwestdeutschland
und Bayern
www.ekd.de/kirche/refore.html

Archiv des Synodalrates der
Evangelisch-Reformierten Kirche in Nordwestdeutschland
und Bayern
Saarstraße 6
D-26789 Leer

also:
Postfach 1380
D-26763 Leer

Rheinland
Evangelische Kirche in Rheinland
www.ekir.de

Evangelische Kirche im Rheinland
Archiv
Hans-Böckler-Straße 7
D-40476 Düsseldorf

Evangelische Kirche im Rheinland
Archiv
Postfach 320340
D-40418 Düsseldorf

Sachsen (Provinz)
Evangelische kirche der Kirchenprovinze Sachsen
www.ekd.de/kps/welcome.htm

Evangelische Kirche der Kirchenprovinze Sachsen
Evangelisches Konsistorium
Am Dom 2
D-3998 Magdet

Sachsen
Evangelisch-Lutherische Landeskirche Sachsens
www.ekd.de/kirche/elksachse.html

Evangelisch-Lutherische Landeskirche Sachsens
Landeskirchenarchiv
Lukasstraße 6
D-01069 Dresden

Schaumburg-Lippe
Evangelisch-Lutherische Landeskirche
Schaumburg-Lippe
www.ekd.de/kirche/schaum.html

Evangelisch-Lutherische
Landeskirche Schaumburg-Lippe
Herderstraße 27
D-31675 Buckeburg

Silesia

Evangelische Kirche der Schlesischen Oberlausitz
www.inf-gr.htw-zittau.de/eksol/eksol/htm

Evangelische Kirche der Schlesischen Oberlausitz
Konsistorium
Schlautrother Straße 11
D-02827 Görlitz

Thüringen

Evangelisch-Lutherische Kirche in Thüringen
www.ekd.de/kirche/thuere.html

Evangelisch-Lutherische Kirche in Thüringen
Landeskirchliches Archiv
Schloßberg 4a
D-99817 Eisenach

Westfalen

Evangelische Kirche von Westfalen
www.ekvw.de

Evangelische Kirche von Westfalen
Landeskirchliches Archiv
Altstädter Kirchplatz 5
D-33602 Bielefeld

Evangelische Kirche von Westfalen
Landeskirchliches Archiv
Postfach 101051
D-33510 Bielefeld

Württemberg
Evangelische Landeskirche in Württemberg
www.elk-wue.de

Evangelische Landeskirche in Württemberg
Landeskirchliches Archiv
Gänsheidestraße 4
D-70184 Stuttgart

Evangelische Landeskirche in Württemberg
Landeskirchliches Archiv
Postfach 101342
D-70012 Stuttgart

CATHOLIC CHURCH

Catholic church (Katholische Kirche) records in Germany are arranged by ecclesiastical divisions. Each parish (pfarr) is overseen by a bishopric (bistum) which is in turn overseen by an archbishop (erzbistum). The following lists include the various Bishoprics (bistum) and Archbishoprics (erzbistum) with their corresponding physical addresses and their Internet addresses where available.

Katholische Kirche in Deutschland
http://www.kath.de

Bistum Aachen
http://www.bistum-aachen.de

Bistum Eischstätt
http://www.ku-eichstaett.de/BISTUM/

Diöesanarchiv Eichstätt
Luitpoldstraße 1

D-85072 Eichstätt/Bayern
Ph: 08421/50411

Bistum Essen
http://www.bistum-essen.de

Bistum Erfurt
http://www.kath.de/bistum/erfurt/index.htm
Archiv des Bischöflischen Amtes Erfurt-Meiningen
Hermanusplatz 9
D-99084 Erfurt
Ph: 0361-24595

Bistum Fulda
http://www.bistum.fulda.net
Bistumsarchiv Fulda
Bischöfliches Generalvikariat
Paulustor 5
D-36037 Fulda

Bistum Hildesheim
Bistumsarchiv des Bistums Hildesheim
Pfaffenstieg 2
D-31134 Hildesheim

also:
Postfach 100263
D-31134 Hildesheim

Bistum Limburg
http://www.kath.de/bistum/limburg.index.htm
Diözesanarchiv Limburg
Roßmarkt 4
D-65549 Limburg

Bistum Magdeburg
http://www.kath.de/bistum/magdeburg/index.htm

Zentralarchiv des Bischöflischen Amtes Magdeburg
Max-Josef-Metzgerstraße 1
D-39104 Magdeburg

Bistum Mainz
http://www.kath.de/bistum/mainz/index.htm

Bistum Osnabrück
http://bistum-osnabrueck.de

Diözesanarchiv des Bistums Osnabrück
Bischöfliches Generalvikariat
Große Domfreiheit 10
D-49074 Osnabrück

Bistum Passau
http://www.bistum-passau.de/home.htm

Archiv des Bistums Passau
Luragogasse 4
D-94032 Passau

Bistum Regensburg

Bischöfliches Zentralarchiv
St. Petersweg 11-13
D-93047 Regensburg

Bistum Rottenberg–Stuttgart
http://www.kirchen.de/dioezesen/drs/drs-inh.html

Bischöfliches Ordinariat, Diözesanarchiv
Bischöfliches Palais
Eugen-Bolz-Platz 1
D-72108 Rottenburg

Bistum Speyer
http://www.kath.de/bistum/speyer.index.htm

Archiv des Bistums Speyer
Kleine Pfaffengasse 16-18
D-67346 Speyer

Bistum Trier (Treves)
http://www.dioezese-trier.de

Bistumsarchiv und Kirchenbuchamt Trier
Jesuitenstraße 13b
D-54290 Trier

Bistum Würzburg
*http://www.bistum-
wuerzburg.de/wuerzburg/wuerzburghome.html*

Erzbistum Bamberg
http://www.erzbistum-bamberg.de

Erzbistum Berlin
http://www.kath.de/bistum/berlin/index.htm

Diözesanarchiv Berlin
Götzstraße 65
12099 Berlin

Erzbistum Freiburg

Erzbischöfliches Archiv Freiburg
Herrenstraße 35
D-79098 Freiburg

Erzbistum München und Freising
http://www.kath.de/bistum/freiburg/index.htm

Archiv des Erzbistums München und Freising
Karmeliterstraße 1
D-80333 München

Erzbistum Paderborn
http://nrw-online.de/kmw

Erzbistumsarchiv Paderborn
Domplatz 3
D-33098 Paderborn

CHAPTER FIVE

ARCHIVAL RECORDS

A RCHIVAL RECORDS IN Germany often are under utilized by beginning researchers because most of these researchers are unfamiliar with the various types of records that may be obtained for an ancestor. Of the records sources discussed earlier, most are located in archives throughout Germany. Due to the very fragmented history of Germany, many different types of archives have been established. These range from church archives to regional or state archives and often include archives for individual family records. In seeking records for your ancestor, remember that archives are, as a rule, established in the larger cities of an area. Many archives do not conduct research by correspondence but can provide you with the names of researchers who can access the records for you.

Baden–Wüerttemberg

Generallandesarchiv Karlsruhe
Nördliche Hildapromenade 2
D-76133 Karlsruhe

Hauptstaatsarchiv Stuttgart
Konrad-Adenauer-Straße 4
D-70173 Stuttgart

Staatsarchiv Freiburg
Colombiastraße 4
D-79098 Freiburg

Staatsarchiv Ludwigsburg
Schloß Ludwigsburg
Schloßstraße 30
D-71634 Ludwigsburg

Staatsarchiv Sigmaringen
Strohdorfer Straße 11
D-72488 Sigmaringen

Staatsarchiv Wertheim
Bronnbach 19
D-97877 Wertheim

Bayern

Sudetendeutsches Genealogisches Archiv
Erikaweg 58
D-93053 Regensburg

Zentralstelle der Heimatsortskarteien
Lessingstraße 1
D-80336 München

Bayerisches Hauptstaatsarchiv
Schönfeldstraße 5
D-80539 München

Staatsarchiv München
Schönfeldstraße 3
D-80539 München

Staatsarchiv Augsburg
Salomon-Idler-Straße 2
D-86159 Augsburg

Staatsarchiv Landshut
Burg Trausnitz
D-84036 Landshut

Staatsarchiv Amberg
Archivstraße 3
D-92224 Amberg

Staatsarchiv Nürnberg
Archivstraße 17
D-90408 Nürnberg

Staatsarchiv Würzburg
Residenzplatz 2
D-97070 Würzburg

Staatsarchiv Bamberg
Hainstraße 39
D-96047 Bamberg

Staatsarchiv Coburg
Herrngasse 11
D-96450 Coburg

Brandenburg

Brandenburgisches Landeshauptarchiv Potsdam
Sanssouci-Orangerie
D-14469 Potsdam

Geheimes Staatsarchiv Preussischer Kulturbesitz
Archivstraße 12-14
D-14195 Berlin

Elsaß-Lothringen (Alsace-Lorraine)

Archives Départementales du Bas-Rhin
5 rue Fischart
67000 Strasbourg FRANCE

Archives Départementales du Haut-Rhin
Cité Administrative
3 rue Fleischhauer
F68026 Colmar cedex, FRANCE

Archives Départementales de Meurthe-et-Moselle
1 rue de la Monnaie
54052 Nancy Cedex FRANCE

Archives Départementales de la Meuse
20 rue Mgr Aimond
55012 Bar-le-Duc FRANCE

Archives Départementales de la Moselle
1 allée du Château
57070 St-Julien-les-Metz FRANCE

Archives Départementales des Vosges
Allée des Hêtres, ZI La Voivre
88000 Epinal FRANCE

Hessen

Hessisches Haupstaatsarchiv
Mosbacherstraße 55
D-65187 Wiesbaden

Hessisches Staatsarchiv Darmstadt Schloß
D-64283 Darmstadt

Kreisarchiv Main-Taunus-Kreis
Bolongarostraße 101
D-65929 Frankfurt am Main

Kreisarchiv für den Odenwaldekreis
Landratsamt, Michelstädter Straße 12
D-64711 Erbach

Hessisches Staatsarchiv Marburg
Friedrichsplatz 15
D-35037 Marburg

Mecklenburg

Staatsarchiv Schwerin
Graf-Schack-Allee 2
D-19053 Schwerin

Landkreis Bad Doberan Kreisarchiv
August-Bebel-Straße 3
D-18209 Bad Doberan

Landkreis Demmin Kreisarchiv
Adolf-Pompe-Straße 12-15
D-17109 Demmin

Landkreis Güstrow Kreisarchiv
D-18273 Güstrow

Landkreis Ludwigslust Kreisarchiv
Alexandrienstraße 576
D-19288 Ludwigslust

Landkreis Mecklenburg-strelitz Kreisarchiv
Bienenweg 1
D-17033 Neubrandenburg

Landkreis Müritz Kreisarchiv
Kietzstraße 10/11
D-17192 Waren

Landkreis Nordvorpommern Kreisarchiv Grimmen
Bahnhofstraße 12/13
D-18507 Grimmen

Landkreis Ostvorpommern Kreisarchiv
Demminer Straße 71-74
D-17389 Anklam

Landkreis Parchim Kreisarchiv
Moltkeplatz 2
D-19370 Parchim

Landkreis Rügen Kreisarchiv
Industriestraße 4
D-18528 Bergen

Grundbucharchiv Schwerin (Central Land Archive)
Lübeckerstraße 287
D-19059 Schwerin

Landkreis Uecker-Randow Kreisarchiv
Am Markt 1
D-17309 Pasewalk

Vorpommersches Landesarchiv Greifswald
Martin-Andersen-Nexö-Platz 1
D-17489 Greifswald

Niedersachsen

Niedersächsisches Hauptstaatsarchiv Hannover
Am Archiv 1
D-30169 Hannover

Niedersächsiches Staatsarchiv in Wolfenbüttel
Forstweg 2
D-38302 Wolfenbüttel

Niedersächsisches Staatsarchiv in Bückeburg
Schloß
D-31675 Bückeburg

also:
Postfach 1350
D-31665 Bückeburg

Niedersächsisches Staatsarchiv in Oldenburg
Damm 43
D-26135 Oldenburg

Niedersächsisches Staatsarchiv in Osnabrück
Schloßstraße 29
D-49074 Osnabrück

Niedersächsisches Staatsarchiv in Aurich
Oldersumer Straße 50
D-26603 Aurich

Rheinland Pfalz

Institut für Pfälzische Geschichte und Volkskunde
Benzinoring 6
D-67637 Kaiserslautern

Oberpfalz

Staatsarchiv Amberg
Archivstraße 3
D-92224 Amberg

Staatsarchiv Landshut
Burg Trausnitz
D-84036 Landshut

Staatsarchiv Nürnberg
Archivstrße 17
D-90408 Nürnberg

Pommern

(Staatsarchiv Köslin)
Archivum Panstwowe w Koszalinie
ul. Zwyciestwa 117
PL-75-601 Koszalin POLAND

(Staatsarchiv Schneidemühl)
Archiwum Panstwowe
Kilinskiego 12
PL-64-920 Pila POLAND

(Staatsarchiv Stettin)
Archivum Panstwowe w Szczecinie
ul. Sw. Wojciecha 13
PL-70-410 Szczecin POLAND

(Staatsarchiv Stolp)
Archiwum Panstwowe
ul. Partyzantówa 31A
PL-72-600 Slupsk POLAND

POLISH ARCHIVES

Catholic Archives

Archiwum Archidieczjalne w Bialymstoku
ul. Warszawska 46
15-077 Bialystok POLAND

Archiwum Diecezjalne w Czestochowie
Al. Najsw. Maryi Panny 54
42-200 Czestochowa POLAND

Archiwum Diecezjalne w Drohiczynie
ul. Koscielna 10
17-312 Drohiczyn POLAND

Archiwum Diecezjalne w Gdansku
ul. CystersÓw 15
80-330 Gdansk POLAND

Archiwum Archidiecezjalne w Gnieznie
Katedra - ul. Kolegiaty 2
62-200 Gniezno POLAND

Archiwum Diecezjalne w Katowicach
ul. Wita Stwosza 16
40-043 Katowice POLAND

Archiwum Diecezjalne w Kielcach
ul. Jana Pawla II 3
25-013 Kielce POLAND

Archiwum Kurii Metropolitalnej w Krakowie
ul. Franciszkanska 3
31-004 Krakow POLAND

Archiwum Archidiecezjalne w Lubaczowie
ul. Adama Mickiewicza 85
37-600 Lubaczow POLAND

Archiwum Diecezjalne w Lublinie
ul. Prymasa Wyszynskiego 2
20-950 Lublin POLAND

Archiwum Diecezjalne w Lomzy
ul. Sadowa 3
18-400 Lomza POLAND

Archiwum Diecezjalne w Lodzi
ul. Ks. Skorupki 3
90-458 Lodz POLAND

Archiwum Diecezjalne w Olsztynie
ul. Kopernika 47
10-512 Olsztyn POLAND

Archiwum Diecezjalne w Opolu
ul. Kardynala Kominka 1a
45-032 Opole POLAND

Archiwum Diecezjalne w Pelplinie
ul. Biskupa K. Dominika 11
83-130 Pelplin POLAND

Archiwum Diecezjalne w Plocku
ul. Abpa Nowowiejskiego 2
09-400 Plock POLAND

Archiwum Archidiecezjalne w Poznaniu
ul. Lubranskiego 1
61-108 Poznan POLAND

Archiwum Diecezjalne w Przemyslu
Pl. Katedralny 4a
37-700 Przemysl POLAND

Archiwum Diecezjalne w Sandomierzu
ul. Sciegiennego 2
27-600 Sandomierz POLAND

Archiwum Diecezjalne w Siedlcach
ul. Swierczewskiego 62
08-100 Siedlce POLAND

Archiwum Diecezji Szczecinsko-Kamienskiej
Pl. Katedralny 8
72-400 Kamien Pomorski POLAND

Archiwum Diecezjalne w Tarnowie
ul. Katedralna 3
33-100 Tarnow POLAND

Archiwum Archidieczjalne w Warszawie
ul. Swietojanska 8
00-288 Warszawa POLAND

Archiwum Diecezjalne we Wloclawku
ul. Gdanska 2/4
87-800 Wloclawek POLAND

Archiwum Archidiecezjalne we Wroclawiu
ul. Kanonia 12
50-328 Wroclaw POLAND

Archiwum Diecezjalne w Zielonej GÓrze
Pl. PowstancÓw Wlkp. 1
65-075 Zielona Gora POLAND

Lutheran Archive

Archiwum Kosciola Ewangelicko-Augsburskiego (Lutheran Church)
ul. Miodowa 21
00-246 Warszawa POLAND

National Archive (pre-World War II records)

Archiwum Glówne Akt Dawnych
ul. Dluga 7
00-263 Warszawa POLAND
(National repository for documents produced prior to 1945)

Regional Archives

Archiwum Panstwowe w Bialymstoku
Rynek T. Kosciuszki 41
15-950 Bialystok POLAND

Archiwum Panstwowe w Bydgoszczy
ul. Dworcowa 65
85-009 Bydgoszcz POLAND
Archiwum Panstwowe w Elblagu
ul. Staroscinska 1
82-200 Malbork POLAND

Archiwum Panstwowe w Gdansku
ul. Waly Piastowskie 5
80-958 Gdansk POLAND

Archiwum Panstwowe w Jeleniej GÓrze
ul. Podwale 27
58-500 Jelenia Gora POLAND

Archiwum Panstwowe w Kaliszu
ul. Zlota 43
62-800 Kalisz POLAND

Archiwum Panstwowe w Katowicach
ul. Józefowska 104
40-145 Katowice POLAND

Archiwum Panstwowe w Kielcach
ul. Warszawska 17
25-953 Kielce POLAND

Archiwum Panstwowe w Koszalinie
ul. Zwyciestwa 117
75-601 Koszalin POLAND

Archiwum Panstwowe w Krakowie
ul. Sienna 16
31-041 Krakow POLAND

Archiwum Panstwowe w Lesznie
ul. Boleslawa Chrobrego 32
64-100 Leszno POLAND

Archiwum Panstwowe w Lublinie
ul. Jezuicka 13
20-950 Lublin POLAND

Archiwum Panstwowe w Lodzi
Plac Wolnosci 1
91-950 Lodz POLAND

Archiwum Panstwowe w Olsztynie
ul. Partyzantow 18
10-521 Olsztyn POLAND

Archiwum Panstwowe w Opolu
ul. Zamkowa 2
45-016 Opole POLAND

Archiwum Panstwowe w Piotrkowie Trybunalskim
ul. Torunska 4
97-300 Piotrkow Trybunalski POLAND

Archiwum Panstwowe w Plocku
ul. Kazimierza Wielkiego 9b
09-400 Plock POLAND

Archiwum Panstwowe w Poznaniu
ul. 23 Lutego 41/43
60-967 Poznan POLAND

Archiwum Panstwowe w Przemyslu
ul. Lelewela 4
37-700 Przemysl POLAND

Archiwum Panstwowe w Radomiu
Rynek 1
26-600 Radom POLAND

Archiwum Panstwowe w Rzeszowie
ul. Bóznicza 2
35-969 Rzeszow POLAND

Archiwum Panstwowe w Siedlcach
ul. Biskupa Ignacego Swirskiego 2
08-110 Siedlce POLAND

Archiwum Panstwowe w Slupsku
ul. Lutoslawskiego 17
76-200 Slupsk POLAND

Archiwum Panstwowe w Suwalkach
ul. Kosciuszki 69
16-400 Suwalki POLAND

Archiwum Panstwowe w Szczecinie
ul. Sw. Wojciecha 13
70-410 Szczecin POLAND

Archiwum Panstwowe w Toruniu
Plac Rapackiego 4
87-100 Torun POLAND

Archiwum Panstwowe Miasta Stolecznego Warszawy
ul. Krzywc Kolo 7
00-270 Warszawa POLAND

Archiwum Panstwowe we Wroclawiu
ul. Pomorska 2
50-215 Wroclaw POLAND

Archiwum Panstwowe z Zamosciu
ul. Moranda 4
22-400 Zamosc POLAND

Archiwum Panstwowe w Zielonej GÓrze
ul. Pionierow Lubuskich 53
66-002 Stary Kisielin 31 POLAND

Posen und Silesia (consult Polish Archives)

Sächsisches Staatsarchiv Leipzig (Ostpreussen)

Abteilung Deutsche Zentralstelle für Genealogie
Schongauerstraße 1
D-04321 Leipzig

Sachsen-Anhalt

Landesarchiv Magdeburg
Landeshauptarchiv
Hegelstraße 25
D-39104 Magdeburg

Staatsarchiv Oranienbaum
Schloss Oranienbaum
D-06785 Oranienbaum

Schaumburg-Lippe

Landkreis Schaumburg
Stadtarchiv Stadthagen
D-31655 Stadthagen

also:
Postfach 327
D-31653 Stadthagen

Thuringen

Thüringisches Hauptstaatsarchiv Weimar
Marstallstraße 2
Postfach 2726
D-99408 Weimar

Thüringisches Staatsarchiv Meiningen
Schloß Bibrabau
D-98617 Meiningen

Thüringisches Staatsarchiv Rudolstadt
Schloß Heidecksburg
D-07407 Rudolstadt

Thüringisches Staatsarchiv Greiz
Oberes Schloß 7
D-07973 Greiz

Kreisarchiv Altenburg
Lindenaustraße 9
D-04600 Altenburg

Kreisarchiv Apolda
Bahnhofstraße 44
D-99510 Apolda

Kreisarchiv Arnstadt
Ritterstraße 13
D-99310 Arnstadt

ꝯENEALOGICAL ꝸOCIETIES

G ENEALOGICAL SOCIETIES MAY be among your greatest resources in researching Germany. Society members are acquainted with the types of records available in the area and their locations and accessibility. Members may also be able to assist you in contacting related family members whose ancestors remained in Germany.

Baden-Württemberg

Verein für Familien- und Wappenkunde in
Württemberg und Baden e.V.
Postfach 10 54 41
D-70047 Stuttgart

Landesverein Badische Heimat e.V.
Heilbronner Straße 3
D-75015 Bretten

Bayern

Bayerischer Landesverein für Familienkunde e.V.
Ludwigstraße 14/I
D-80539 München

Gesellschaft für Familienforschung in Franken e.V.
Archivstraße 17
D-90408 Nürnberg

Hessen

Hessische familiengeschichtliche Vereinigung e.V.
Karolinenplatz 3
D-64289 Darmstadt

Familienkundliche Gesellschaft für Nassau und Frankfurt
e.V.
Mosbacher Straße 55
D-65187 Wiesbaden

Arbeitsgemeinschaft der familienkundlichen Gesellschaften
in Hessen
Postfach 10 13 46
D-34013 Kassel

Kurhessen und Waldeck

Gesellschaft für Familienkunde in Kurhessen und Waldeck
e.V.
Postfach 10 13 46
D-34013 Kassel

Niedersachsen

Familienkundliche Kommission für Niedersachsen und
Bremen sowie angrenzende ostfälische Gebiete e.V.
Steinfeldstraße 34
D-30826 Garbsen

Niedersächsischer Landesverein für Familienkunde e.V.
Am Bokemahle 14-16
D-39171 Hannover

Oberpfalz

Gesellschaft für Familienforschung in der Oberpfalz e.V.
Rachelstraße 12
D-93059 Regensburg
Oldenburg

Oldenburgische Gesellschaft für Familienkunde
Lerigauweg 14
D-26131 Oldenburg

Rheinland-Pfalz

Nordrhein-Westfälisches Personenstandsarchiv Rheinland
Schlossstraße 12
D-50321 Brühl

Arbeitsgemeinschaft für Pfälzisch-Rheinische
Familienkunde e.V.
Rottstraße 17
D-67061 Ludwigshafen

Saarland

Arbeitsgemeinschaft für Saarländische Familienkunde e.V.
Hebbelstraße 3
D-66346 Püttlingen

Schleswig-Holstein

Schleswig-Holsteinische Gesellschaft für Familienforschung
und Wappenkunde e.V.
Postfach 3809
D-24037 Kiel

Schwaben

Arbeitskreis donauschwäbischer Familienforscher
Goldmühlestraße 30
D-71065 Sindelfingen

Thüringen

Arbeitsgemeinschaft Genealogie Thüringen e.V.
Martin-Andersen-Nexö-Straße 62
D-99096 Erfurt

Westfalen

Wesrfälische Gesellschaft für Genealogie und
Familienforschung
Postfach 6125
D-48133 Münster

INDEX

Napoleon, 12, 13
Nassau, Duchy of, 14
Nazi party, 16
Netherlands, 10
newspapers, 41
nicknames, 25
North German Confederation,
   14–15

Ⓞ

occupational records, 36–38, 37
online tools, 21–22
Ostfriesland, 25
Otto I, 7

Ⓟ

Palatinate Protestant Union, 10
patronymics, 25
Peasant War, 9
Pepin the Short, 6
place names. *See* location names
Pommerania, 10, 13
Posen, 15
Prussian Empire, 11–12, 13, 14

Ⓡ

Reformation, 9–10
Rhineland, 13
Roman Empire, 4–5
Rudolph I, 8

Ⓢ

Salians, 7–8
Saxe-Weimar, 14
Saxons, 5, 7
Saxony, 13
Saxony, Duchy of, 7
Schleswig, 14, 15
Schleswig-Holstein, 25, 33
school records, 41

Seven Years War, 11
Silesia, 11
spellings, 24
surnames
   naming practices, 25
   spelling errors in, 24
Swabia, Duchy of, 7
Swabians, 5
Switzerland, 10

Ⓣ

tax lists, 41
Teutonic Knights, 8–9
Thirty Years War, 10–11
towns, importance in German
   research, 3
Treaty of Prague, 14
Treaty of Verdun, 6

Ⓤ

vital records
   church parish registers as, 29–32
   civil registration of, 12, 29, 35

Ⓦ

Weimar Republic, 15–16
Westfalen, 13
West Franks, 6–7
West Germany, 16–17
West Prussia, 11–12, 15
William II (Kaiser), 15
work records, 36–38, 37
World War I, 15
World War II, 16
Wüerttemberg, 14, 35